Press Release Mastery

A Small Business Owner's Guide to Gaining Local Media Attention

Jeremy Lesniak

wK Books

What is This Book and Who is it for?

Welcome, small business owners! This book is your gateway to mastering press releases, an often overlooked yet powerful tool in your marketing arsenal. Whether you run a charming local bakery, a budding tech startup, or a neighborhood bookstore, this guide is designed specifically for you. It's for those who are stepping into the realm of press releases for the first time and for those who have tried them but haven't quite cracked the code to their full potential.

In these pages, you'll find a practical, easy-to-follow roadmap that demystifies the art of crafting and using press releases effectively. If you've ever wondered how to grab the attention of local media or how to turn a simple announcement into a newsworthy story, you're in the right place.

How is This Book Different from Others?

In a sea of marketing guides and how-to books, this one stands out for its brevity, clarity, and practicality. As a small business owner, you're already wearing multiple hats, managing a tight schedule. You need concise, actionable advice that gets straight to the point without the fluff. This book is designed to be like a focused, insightful chat over coffee – valuable insights packed into a brief, digestible format.

Why trust this guide? Because, like you, I value time and effective, straightforward advice. I've navigated the often-confusing landscape of press releases, learning through experience, and refining strategies that work. In this book, I've distilled these insights to share with you.

Through clear explanations, step-by-step guidance, and practical tips, we'll explore how to craft press releases that resonate with your audience and the media. This isn't just about sending out information; it's about telling your story in a way that captivates and engages, helping your business gain the visibility and recognition it deserves.

Let's embark on this journey together, unlocking the potential of press releases to elevate your business's reach and impact.

Table of Contents

Press Release Mastery

A Small Business Owner's Guide to Gaining Local Media Attention

Summary

Introduction

In the bustling world of small business, effective communication is key. This guide is your companion in mastering the art of press releases, a powerful tool often underutilized in the small business sector. It's tailored to help you, the small business owner, navigate the landscape of local media attention, with practical, actionable advice.

Section 1: Understanding Press Releases

- **Key Concepts**: A press release is more than just an announcement; it's a story told to the media with the goal of gaining publicity.

- **Newsworthiness**: Learn to identify what makes a story newsworthy and how to craft your press release to capture the media's attention.

- **Detailed Guide**: We delve into the art of finding compelling angles for your stories, ensuring they resonate with your target audience and the media.

Section 2: Building a Local Media List

- **Importance of Targeting**: A well-researched media list is crucial. It's about quality, not quantity.

- **Creating Your List**: Discover how to build a media list that aligns with your business's niche and target audience.

- **Maintenance and Update**: Understand the dynamics of media outlets and how to keep your list relevant and effective.

- **Non-Advertising Format**: Press releases should inform, not sell. Learn the difference to avoid being dismissed as just another advertisement.

- **Structure and Content**: Get a grip on the standard press release format, from engaging headlines to the informative body and the essential boilerplate.

- **Deep Dive**: We guide you through each element of the press release, ensuring clarity and impact while adhering to journalistic standards.

Section 4: Crafting Content That Matters

- **Resonance with Public**: Your content should not only be relevant but also engaging and informative.

- **What to Include**: A concise guide on the essential elements of an effective press release.

- **Tips and Tricks**: From writing style to content focus, learn how to avoid common pitfalls and make your press release stand out.

Section 5: Maximizing Press Release Impact

- **Beyond the Release**: A press release is a starting point, not the end. Learn to leverage it across different marketing channels.

- **Integration Strategies**: Combine your press release efforts with email and social media for broader impact.

- **Comprehensive Approach**: We cover strategies for amplifying your press release's reach, timing it effectively, and maximizing its lifecycle.

- **Follow-Up**: Tips on how to follow up with media outlets to boost your press release's effectiveness.

- **Digital Distribution**: Best practices for digitally distributing your press release to maximize reach and impact.

- **Measuring Success**: Understand how to measure the impact of your press release and adjust your strategy accordingly.

Checklists

- **Media List Maintenance**: A step-by-step checklist to keep your media contacts organized and up to date.

- **Press Release Lifecycle**: From conception to leveraging, a checklist covering the entire journey of your press release.

Conclusion

This guide concludes with a call to action for small business owners to start their journey in the world of press releases. With the tools and knowledge provided in this book, you are well-equipped to create impactful press releases that resonate with your audience and garner local media attention.

Part 1: What is a Press Release and Its Purpose?

A press release is a written communication that reports specific but brief information about an event, circumstance, or other happening. It's typically tied to a business or organization and is provided to the media through various means. The ultimate purpose? To announce something ostensibly newsworthy.

Fundamentally, a press release serves two main purposes: to share information that your business considers important and to grab the attention of journalists or media outlets so they spread your message further. This could be anything from launching a new product, opening a new branch, a significant business change, or responding to a public issue.

Part 2: Identifying Newsworthy Topics for a Press Release

Identifying a newsworthy topic for a press release is crucial. Not everything your business does warrants a press release, but certain events or announcements can catch the media's eye:

1. *Major Company Changes*: Announcements about mergers, acquisitions, or leadership changes.

2. *New Products or Services*: Launching something novel or significantly improved.

3. *Events*: Hosting or participating in a community or industry event.

4. *Awards or Accolades*: Recognition your business has received.

5. *Significant Milestones:* Celebrating anniversaries or achieving major goals.

6. *Expert Insights*: Offering professional perspectives on industry trends or news.

7. *Community Involvement*: Participating in charity work or local community events.

These topics generally share common traits: uniqueness, timeliness, relevance, and impact. They should be of interest not just to your organization but to your intended audience.

Part 3: Detailed Guidance on Finding Newsworthy Angles

Finding a newsworthy angle is about looking at your information from a journalist's or reader's perspective. What about your news would interest them? Here are some tips:

1. *Timeliness*: News is about what's happening now. Your press release should be current and contain up-to-date information.

2. *Relevance*: Your story should be relevant to your target audience. Tailor your press release to fit the interests of the media outlet and its audience.

3. *Impact*: Your news should have significance or impact. How does it affect your industry, community, or target audience?

4. *Human Interest*: Adding a human element can make your press release more relatable. Personal stories, quotes, or experiences can add depth.

5. *Uniqueness*: What makes your story stand out? Highlight what's different about your news.

6. *Clarity and Concision*: Be clear and concise in your writing. Journalists are busy; make it easy for them to understand and use your story.

7. *Visuals*: Whenever possible, include visuals. Photos, videos, or infographics can make your press release more engaging.

8. *Brainstorming Topics*: Regularly brainstorm with your team. Discuss different aspects of your business and how they might be newsworthy. Stay aware of industry trends, as they can offer opportunities for commentary or insights.

By focusing on these elements, you can craft press releases that are not only informative but also compelling and likely to be picked up by media outlets. Remember, the goal is to provide value to both the journalist and their audience, making your news worth reading and sharing.

Part 1: The Importance of a Targeted Media List

A targeted media list is a cornerstone of effective press release distribution. It's not just about sending your press release to as many contacts as possible; it's about sending it to the right ones. A well-crafted media list ensures that your press release reaches the people who are most likely to be interested in and publish your news.

The right media contacts can amplify your message, reaching a broader audience and potentially even leading to more media opportunities. This list should include journalists, editors, reporters, and broadcasters who cover topics related to your business or industry.

Part 2: Creating Your Media List – A One-Page Summary

1. *Identify Your Target Audience*: Understand who you want to reach with your press release. This will guide you in selecting the appropriate media outlets.

2. *Research Relevant Media Outlets*: Look for local newspapers, magazines, blogs, radio stations, and TV stations that cover topics related to your business or industry.

3. *Find Contact Information*: Once you've identified relevant media outlets, find contact information for editors, reporters, or journalists. This information is often available on the outlet's website.

4. *Segment Your List*: Organize your list by media type, geographic location, or area of interest. This makes it easier to send targeted press releases in the future.

5. *Keep It Updated*: Media contacts frequently change jobs or beats. Regularly update your list to ensure it remains accurate.

Part 3: In-Depth Guide to Media List Building

Building a comprehensive and effective media list is a multi-step process:

1. *Define Your Goals*: What do you hope to achieve with your press release? This will help in identifying the most relevant media outlets.

2. *Conduct Thorough Research*: Beyond just Googling, consider using media databases, social media, and industry publications to find the right contacts. Attend industry events and network to get to know the local media.

3. *Understand the Media Landscape*: Familiarize yourself with the work of the journalists and outlets you add to your list. Understanding their interests and style can help tailor your press release to suit their audience.

4. *Create a Database*: Use a spreadsheet or a CRM tool to organize your media contacts. Include names, titles, contact information, and any notes on their interests or past interactions.

5. *Quality over Quantity*: It's better to have a smaller list of highly relevant contacts than a large list of generic ones. Focus on building relationships with key journalists who are most likely to be interested in your news.

6. *Personalize Your Approach*: When you reach out to your media contacts, personalize your communication. Refer to their recent articles or segments that align with your press release.

7. *Regular Maintenance*: Regularly review and update your media list. Remove contacts who no longer cover relevant topics, and add new ones you discover.

By meticulously building and maintaining your media list, you increase the chances of your press release being noticed and published, helping to get your message out to the right audience effectively.

Section 3: Formatting Your Press Release

Part 1: The Non-Advertising Format of Press Releases

Press releases are informational and newsworthy, distinct from advertising material. Their purpose is to inform media outlets and the public about significant events or developments in your business, not to overtly sell a product or service. The key is to present information in a way that's compelling to journalists, who may then decide to share it with their audience.

The format of a press release helps to achieve this goal. It's structured to provide essential information quickly and efficiently, making it easy for journalists to understand your message and its significance.

Part 2: The Standard Press Release Format – A One-Page Summary

1. *Headline*: This should grab attention and clearly convey the main point of the release. Make it engaging and succinct.

2. *Dateline*: Includes the release date and originating city of the press release.

3. *Introduction*: In the first paragraph, answer the who, what, when, where, and why. This part should sum up the most critical aspects of the release.

4. *Body*: Here, elaborate on the details. Provide background information, quotes from key stakeholders or experts, and any additional relevant data that supports your main message.

5. *Boilerplate*: A short paragraph about your company, providing background information for journalists.

6. *Contact Information*: Provide the name, phone number, and email address of the person who can answer further questions about the release.

7. *End Mark*: A simple "###" or "-END-" to indicate the end of the press release.

1. *Crafting a Compelling Headline*: Your headline should be clear, interesting, and provide a hook. It's the first thing a journalist sees, so it needs to make a strong impression.

2. *Writing the Introduction*: This is where you get to the heart of the story. Make sure the first paragraph succinctly covers the essential information: who is involved, what is happening, where and when it's happening, and why it matters.

3. *Developing the Body*:

   - <u>Expand on Details:</u> After the introduction, go into more detail about your news.

   - <u>Use Quotes</u>: Include quotes from key figures in your business or industry to add credibility and a personal touch.

   - <u>Include Statistics or Data</u>: If applicable, data can bolster your claims and add substance to your release.

4. *Boilerplate Information*: This should provide a brief overview of your company. Include your mission, the services or products you offer, and any notable achievements or recognitions.

5. *Contact Information*: Make it easy for journalists to reach out for more information. Include the contact person's name, direct phone number, and email address.

6. *Formatting Tips*:

  - Keep it concise, usually one page.

  - Write in the third person.

  - Use a professional, journalistic tone.

  - Avoid jargon and industry-specific terms that might not be
    widely understood.

7. *Proofreading*: Always proofread your press release for
grammar, spelling, and factual accuracy. Mistakes can
undermine credibility and professionalism.

Creating a well-formatted, engaging, and informative press
release is crucial for capturing the media's attention and getting
your news published. By adhering to these guidelines, you can
effectively communicate your message and enhance your
business's public relations efforts.

Part 1: Creating Content that Resonates with the Public

The content of your press release should resonate with both the media and your target audience. It's not just about relaying facts; it's about telling a story that connects on a human level. Your goal is to craft a narrative that is engaging, relevant, and informative. Remember, the media is more likely to cover your story if it appeals to their readers, viewers, or listeners.

Part 2: Key Elements to Include in a Press Release – A One-Page Summary

1. *Compelling Story*: Focus on why your news matters. What's the human interest angle? How does it impact your audience or the community?

2. *Clear Objectives*: Define what you want to achieve with your press release. Are you trying to inform, educate, announce, or respond to something?

3. *Factual Information*: Include all relevant facts like dates, statistics, and background information. Accuracy is crucial.

4. *Relevant Quotes*: Add quotes from key people involved in the story. This could be the CEO, industry experts, or stakeholders. Quotes add a personal touch and credibility.

5. *Supporting Data*: If applicable, include data or research to back up your statements. This can be survey results, market data, or other relevant statistics.

6. *Call to Action*: If appropriate, include a call to action. What do you want readers to do after reading your press release?

7. *Multimedia Elements*: If possible, include high-quality images, videos, or infographics. These elements can increase the likelihood of your press release getting noticed.

Part 3: Detailed Advice on Writing Techniques and Content Creation

1. *Finding the Right Angle*: Every story has multiple angles. Find the one that best aligns with your audience's interests and your objectives.

2. *Writing for Clarity*: Use clear, concise language. Avoid jargon and technical terms that might be confusing to a general audience.

3. *Emphasizing Newsworthiness*: Highlight what's new or different. Why is this story important now?

4. *Building a Narrative*: Good storytelling is key. Create a narrative that flows logically and keeps the reader engaged.

5. *Incorporating Visuals*: People are drawn to visuals. Include relevant photos or graphics that enhance your story and make it more shareable.

6. *Avoiding Common Pitfalls*:

  - Don't make it too promotional. Focus on the news aspect rather than selling.

  - Avoid overstating or exaggerating claims.

  - Be cautious with humor or puns, which can be misinterpreted or seen as unprofessional.

7. *Leveraging Social Proof*: Mention any partnerships, endorsements, or connections to well-known entities or individuals if relevant and appropriate.

8. *Cultural and Social Sensitivity*: Be aware of cultural and social nuances. Ensure your content is respectful and considerate of diverse audiences.

9. *SEO Considerations*: If your press release will be distributed online, consider SEO. Use relevant keywords naturally to improve search visibility.

10. *Final Review*: Have someone else review your press release. A fresh pair of eyes can catch errors and provide feedback on clarity and impact.

By focusing on these elements and techniques, your press release will not only inform but also engage and connect with your intended audience, increasing the likelihood of media pickup and public interest.

Part 1: Leveraging a Press Release for Broader Marketing Efforts

The journey of your press release doesn't end with its distribution. To maximize its impact, integrate it into your broader marketing strategy. A well-executed press release can enhance your brand's visibility, reinforce your marketing messages, and complement your other marketing efforts, such as social media, email marketing, and even SEO.

Part 2: Integrating Press Releases with Other Marketing Channels – A One-Page Summary

1. *Social Media*: Share your press release on your social media channels. Tailor the message to fit each platform and engage with your followers about the news.

2. *Email Marketing*: Include a summary or link to your press release in your email newsletters. It's an excellent way to keep your existing customers informed and engaged.

3. *Website*: Create a dedicated news or press section on your website where you can post all your press releases. This increases the accessibility of your news to visitors and can aid in SEO.

4. *Blogging*: Write a blog post that expands on your press release topic, providing more in-depth information, commentary, or background stories.

5. *Networking*: Use the content of your press release as talking points in networking events or industry conferences.

6. *Customer Engagement*: Inform your customers about your press release in-store or through direct communication if it's relevant to their interests.

7. Media Follow-Up: After sending out your press release, follow up with key media contacts. A personal follow-up can increase the chances of your story being picked up.

Part 3: Comprehensive Strategies for Amplifying Your Press Release

1. *Timing is Crucial*: Release your news when it's most relevant. Consider industry events, seasons, or current trends that might impact the interest in your story.

2. *Build Relationships with Journalists*: Cultivate ongoing relationships with journalists and influencers in your field. They are more likely to cover your story if they know and trust your brand.

3. *Utilize Online Distribution Services*: These services can broaden the reach of your press release to a wider audience and can be particularly beneficial for online visibility.

4. *Measure and Analyze Impact*: Use tools to track how your press release performs. Look at website traffic, media pickup, social media engagement, and any direct inquiries or sales that result from the release.

5. *Repurpose Content*: Use the information from your press release to create infographics, videos, or social media content. This helps to reinforce your message across various platforms.

6. *SEO Benefits*: Include relevant keywords in your press release to improve your website's search engine ranking. However,

ensure that the use of keywords is natural and doesn't detract from the quality of the content.

7. *Leverage Local Angles*: If your news has a local component, emphasize this when reaching out to local media outlets. Local stories are more likely to get picked up.

8. *Continuous Learning*: Analyze what works and what doesn't. Each press release is an opportunity to refine your approach based on the responses and results you get.

By integrating these strategies, your press release can serve as a powerful tool in your overall marketing plan, extending its reach and effectiveness far beyond its initial release.

After sending out your press release, following up with media outlets can significantly increase the chances of your story being covered. Here are some effective tips for following up:

1. *Wait for the Right Time*: Give journalists enough time to review your press release. Typically, waiting for 2-3 days after sending it is advisable. Avoid following up too soon or too often, as this can be seen as pushy.

2. *Choose the Right Method*: Email is usually the best way to follow up. It's less intrusive than a phone call and gives journalists time to respond at their convenience. However, if you have an existing relationship with a journalist, a phone call might be more effective.

3. *Be Brief and Professional*: Your follow-up message should be concise. Reiterate the key points of your press release and express your willingness to provide additional information or answer questions.

4. *Personalize Your Communication*: Address the journalist by name and reference any past interactions if applicable. Personalization shows that you've done your research and are not just sending generic follow-ups.

5. *Offer Additional Value*: If possible, offer new angles or additional information that was not included in the original press release. This might spark the journalist's interest.

6. *Be Respectful of Their Time*: Journalists are often busy with tight deadlines. Be respectful of their time. If they express disinterest or say they're busy, thank them for their time and ask if you can contact them in the future.

7. *Use Social Media Judiciously*: If you're connected with the journalist on social media, engaging with their content can be a subtle way to remind them of your press release. However, avoid direct messaging unless you have an established social media relationship.

8. *Prepare for Questions*: Be ready to answer questions or provide additional details about your press release. Quick and thorough responses can make a difference in getting your story covered.

9. *Thank Them for Their Time*: Regardless of the outcome, always thank the journalist for considering your press release. Building a courteous professional relationship can benefit future interactions.

10. *Keep Track of Responses*: Keep a record of who you've followed up with and their responses. This information can be valuable for tailoring your approach in future communications.

11. *Learn from Each Interaction*: Use each follow-up as a learning opportunity. Note what works and what doesn't, and adjust your strategies accordingly for future press releases.

Remember, the goal of following up is not just to secure immediate coverage but also to build lasting relationships with media professionals that can benefit your business in the long run.

In the digital age, the distribution of press releases has evolved significantly. Leveraging digital channels effectively can greatly enhance the reach and impact of your press release. Here are some best practices for digital press release distribution:

1. *Utilize Online Distribution Services*: Platforms like PR Newswire, Business Wire, or PRWeb can distribute your press release to a wide network of media outlets, journalists, and online news aggregators. Choose a service that aligns with your industry and target audience.

2. *Optimize for Search Engines (SEO)*: Use relevant keywords in your press release to improve its visibility in search engine results. However, ensure that the use of keywords feels natural and does not compromise the quality of the content.

3. *Incorporate Multimedia Elements*: Digital press releases can be enhanced with images, videos, infographics, and links. These elements can make your release more engaging and shareable online.

4. *Leverage Social Media*: Share your press release on your company's social media platforms. Tailor the message for each platform and use hashtags to increase visibility.

5. *Targeted Email Distribution*: Send your press release directly to a curated list of media contacts. Personalize your emails to increase the chances of your release being read and considered.

6. *Responsive Design*: Ensure that your digital press release is mobile-friendly. With an increasing number of journalists and readers accessing content on mobile devices, a responsive design is crucial.

7. *Track and Analyze Performance*: Use analytics tools to track how your press release performs. Look at metrics like views, shares, engagement, and website traffic driven by the release.

8. *Timing Matters*: Publish and distribute your press release at a time when it's most likely to be noticed. Avoid weekends and major holidays. Early in the week and mornings are generally the best times.

9. *Follow-Up Online*: If you have contacts that you've emailed the press release to, a respectful follow-up can be effective. Additionally, engaging with any online discussions or mentions of your press release can further its reach.

10. *Use Anchor Text and Hyperlinks Wisely*: Include hyperlinks to relevant pages on your website. Use descriptive anchor text for these links to improve SEO and provide readers with a clear idea of what to expect when they click.

11. *Consistency in Messaging*: Ensure that the message in your press release aligns with your overall brand messaging and other marketing materials.

12. *Maintain an Online Press Kit*: On your website, maintain a press kit or a dedicated section for press releases. This makes it easier for journalists and interested parties to find and reference your news.

By following these best practices, you can effectively leverage digital platforms for your press release distribution, ensuring a wider reach and greater impact in promoting your news.

Evaluating the success of your press release is essential to understanding its effectiveness and refining future PR strategies. Measuring impact involves assessing both quantitative and qualitative metrics. Here are key ways to measure the impact of your press release:

1. *Media Coverage*: The most direct measure of a press release's success is the amount and quality of media coverage it receives. Track where and how your press release is picked up and mentioned across different media outlets.

2. *Website Traffic*: Use analytics tools to monitor any spikes in website traffic following the distribution of your press release. Pay attention to traffic sources to see if visitors are coming directly from the places where the press release was published.

3. *Engagement Metrics*: If your press release is shared on social media or digital platforms, look at engagement metrics like shares, likes, comments, and mentions. These can indicate how well your audience received your news.

4. *SEO Impact*: Check if your press release has improved your website's search engine ranking for relevant keywords. Increased visibility on search engines can be a significant long-term benefit of press release distribution.

5. *Lead Generation and Sales*: Monitor any increase in inquiries, leads, or sales following the press release. This is especially relevant if the press release was about a new product or service offering.

6. *Social Media Analytics*: Tools like Google Analytics, Hootsuite, or Sprout Social can help track how your press release performs

on social media. Look for changes in follower count, reach, and user engagement.

7. *Sentiment Analysis*: Gauge public sentiment and feedback. Are the responses generally positive, negative, or neutral? This qualitative measure can give you insights into public perception and brand impact.

8. *Influencer and Blogger Mentions*: Track mentions by influencers or bloggers in your industry. Their endorsements can amplify your message and lend credibility to your news.

9. *Email Open and Click-through Rates*: If you've distributed your press release via email, monitor the open and click-through rates to gauge interest and engagement.

10. *Competitor Response*: Observe any responses or competitive moves following your press release, which can indicate its impact on your industry.

11. *Feedback from Journalists*: Direct feedback from journalists or media contacts can provide qualitative insights into how your press release was received and its newsworthiness.

12. *Long-term Effects*: Some impacts, like brand recognition and reputation enhancement, are long-term. Monitor these over time to understand the enduring effects of your press releases.

By regularly measuring these metrics, you can get a comprehensive view of your press release's performance and effectiveness. This data not only helps in assessing the ROI of your current press release but also provides valuable insights for crafting more impactful releases in the future.

Checklist 1: Creating and Maintaining a Media List

Creating and maintaining an effective media list is crucial for the success of your press releases. This checklist will guide you through the process of building and updating a media list that targets the right contacts for your news.

Creating Your Media List:

- [ ] *Define Your Target Audience*: Understand who you want to reach with your press release.

- [ ] *Identify Relevant Media Outlets*: Research media outlets (newspapers, TV/radio stations, online media) that align with your target audience.

- [ ] *Find Individual Contacts*: Look for specific journalists, editors, or reporters who cover topics related to your press release.

- [ ] *Gather Contact Information*: Collect email addresses, phone numbers, and social media handles.

- [ ] *Segment Your List*: Organize your list by media type, beat, or geographic location for targeted distribution.

- [ ] *Verify the Accuracy*: Ensure the contact information is current and accurate.

- [ ] *Regular Updates*: Periodically review and update the list to account for changes in media contacts and outlets.

- [ ] *Track Responses*: Note the responsiveness of contacts to your press releases for future reference.

- [ ] *Expand Your List*: Continuously look for new contacts to add, especially when expanding into new markets or sectors.

- [ ] *Personalize Relationships*: Keep notes on individual preferences or past interactions to personalize future communications.

- [ ] *Monitor Media Moves*: Stay aware of journalists changing jobs or beats, which is common in the media industry.

- [ ] *Engage on Social Media*: Follow and engage with media contacts on social media platforms to build rapport.

- [ ] *Feedback Analysis*: After press release distribution, analyze which contacts engaged with your content and update your list accordingly.

- [ ] *Legal Compliance*: Ensure that your list complies with data protection laws and regulations, like GDPR if applicable.

- [ ] *Tailor Your Pitch*: Customize your press release or pitch to align with the specific interests of the contacts on your list.

- [ ] *Track Distribution*: Keep a record of when and to whom you send each press release.

- [ ] *Evaluate Performance*: Post-release, evaluate which segments of your media list generated the most engagement and adjust your strategy if needed.

By regularly following this checklist, your media list will become a valuable asset in your PR toolkit, helping you to effectively reach the right people with your press releases.

Idea and Planning

- [ ] *Brainstorm Topics*: Identify potential newsworthy topics relevant to your business and audience.

- [ ] *Define Objectives*: Clearly outline what you aim to achieve with the press release.

- [ ] *Research and Gather Information*: Collect all necessary data, statistics, quotes, and resources needed for your press release.

- [ ] *Identify Target Audience*: Determine who the press release is intended for and tailor the content accordingly.

Writing the Press Release

- [ ] *Draft Content*: Write the initial draft of the press release, ensuring it includes all key messages.

- [ ] *Incorporate SEO*: Include relevant keywords to optimize for search engines, if applicable.

- [ ] *Review and Edit*: Revise the draft for clarity, accuracy, and impact. Ensure it adheres to the standard press release format.

- [ ] *Get Approval*: Have all necessary stakeholders review and approve the final version.

Distribution

- [ ] *Select Distribution Channels*: Decide where and how to distribute the press release (e.g., email, online distribution services, direct to journalists).

- [ ] *Prepare Media List*: Update your media list to ensure it includes relevant contacts for this release.

- [ ] *Send Out the Press Release*: Distribute the press release according to your chosen channels and media list.

Follow-Up

- [ ] *Media Outreach*: Conduct follow-up communications with key media contacts to encourage coverage.

- [ ] *Monitor Pickup*: Track where and how your press release is being picked up and mentioned.

- [ ] *Engage on Social Media*: Share the press release on your social media channels and engage with any responses or discussions.

Measuring Success

- [ ] *Analyze Media Coverage*: Assess the extent and quality of media coverage received.

- [ ] *Review Web Analytics*: If applicable, evaluate changes in web traffic or engagement metrics on your website.

- [ ] *Evaluate Social Media Impact*: Look at shares, comments, likes, and other engagement metrics on social media.

- [ ] *Gather Feedback*: Collect and analyze feedback from internal teams, stakeholders, or the audience to gauge reception.

- [ ] *Document Learnings*: Note what worked well and areas for improvement for future press releases.

By methodically following these steps, you can effectively manage the entire process of creating, distributing, and leveraging a press release for your business.

As we conclude this guide on press releases for small business owners, it's important to reflect on the journey we've taken together. From understanding the basics of what makes a press release to mastering the art of crafting and distributing impactful news about your business, we've covered a breadth of strategies and insights designed to elevate your company's public profile.

Embrace the Power of Press Releases: Remember, a well-crafted press release can be a powerful tool in your marketing arsenal. It's not just about disseminating information; it's about telling your story in a way that resonates with your audience and the media. Whether it's launching a new product, announcing a significant milestone, or sharing insights on industry trends, your press release can significantly influence how your business is perceived.

Continuous Learning and Adaptation: The landscape of media and public relations is ever-evolving. Stay adaptable, keep learning, and be ready to tweak your approach based on the changing dynamics of media consumption and communication technologies.

Building Relationships: Developing and nurturing relationships with media professionals is crucial. Your efforts in creating a targeted media list, personalizing your pitches, and following up respectfully can lead to valuable long-term connections.

Measuring and Reflecting: Make a habit of measuring the impact of your press releases and reflecting on the outcomes. Use these insights to refine your future strategies, ensuring that each press release is more effective than the last.

Your Story Matters: As a small business owner, you have unique stories to tell. Your passion, dedication, and hard work are what set you apart. Use press releases to share these stories, connect with your community, and grow your brand.

In closing, I encourage you to take these learnings and apply them with confidence. The world of media relations is rich with opportunity, and by effectively utilizing press releases, you can open new doors for your business. Here's to your success in gaining the attention and recognition your business deserves.

Thank you for embarking on this journey to master the art of the press release. May your stories find their audience and your business flourish in the spotlight it deserves.

We Want to Hear from You!

Reviews are an important part of how others find our books, and they help us create content you love. If you enjoyed this book, please visit the associated Amazon product listing and leave us a review. We will use your feedback to help create more content catered towards you, our loyal readers.

Thank you!!

DON'T MISS OUR EVENTS!

ALL-IN WEEKEND

This 2-day martial arts event will be half training experience and half retreat. The cost of the event includes all of your training, your lodging, food, and an event shirt. All you have to do is show up, and we'll take care of the rest.

FREE TRAINING DAY

whistlekick's Free Training Day is exactly what the name says - one day of the year where martial artists come together to share and learn, all for free. There is no admission fee at this event, instructors are not paid, and whistlekick picks up the tab for the venue and any other logistical costs.

MARTIAL SUMMIT

Martial Summit is our vision for the future. A place where martial artists, from all over the world, of all systems and styles, come together to share. This 4-day event includes Free Training Day Northeast as well as the Never Settle Awards Banquet.

Follow the QR codes above or visit whistlekick.com and click on "For Individuals" to find all the latest info on our incredible events!

Available Now from whistlekick Books

Find it on Amazon!

12 Months to Health

This book is designed to help you establish and reinforce 12 simple, inexpensive habits to achieve a healthier you in 12 months.

Visit us in our Facebook group for more:
https://www.facebook.com/groups/12mth

"Mr. Lesniak has laid out a well-researched, simple, and gradual guide to real success in incorporating healthy habits into one's daily life. I look forward to sharing this with my patients as a partner in their journey toward better health."

— Joshua Singer, Licensed Acupuncturist at River Street Wellness, Montpelier, Vermont

"Setting just the right goal is hard to do, and starting with consistent, bite-sized, achievable goals is the way to achieve real change in your health."

— Irvin Eisenberg, Masters in Occupational Therapy, Structural Integrator and Owner of Resilience Occupational Therapy

"Our healthcare system, as it is built, right now, is largely not designed to help you until AFTER chronic disease strikes. Even preventative health endorsed by your doctor is left to the small choices you make daily, by yourself, well outside of the walls of the clinic."

— Joshua T. White, MD, MBA, Chief Medical Officer, Gifford Medical Center

"12 things that ANYONE can do that will make a vast difference to their life."

— Daniel Eagles

"A single focus for a month makes it much more likely that I will be able to make sustainable changes."

— StaciAnne KaeLeigh Grove

FREE whistlekick Flexibility Program!

Yes, I said FREE! This program is designed by and for martial artists with features you won't find in any other program, at any price. The Flexibility Program is rooted in the latest science, immensely effective, and different from what most of us were taught.

The FREE whistlekick 30-Day Challenge

The program is a FREE and COMPLETE standalone training program you can start at any time. It's designed to be done on its own, without other strength or conditioning programs. The daily workouts can be completed in about 10 minutes, require NO EQUIPMENT, and can be done in a small indoor space.

This program combines martial arts and fitness to get you the exact workout you need on that day. It helps you build momentum to gain more out of your time – with your health, fitness, training, and the rest of your life.

These are just a sample of the programs we offer!

Looking to increase your speed? How about your fighting endurance? Visit whistlekick.com to see how we are revolutionizing the way you train to improve not only your martial arts skills, but also your overall health.

Check out the collection of whistlekick Programs in the whistlekick Store today!

Want to Find More?

You may wish to check out one of our other titles, including *The Martial Artist's Handbook*, an introduction to topics related to practicing martial arts for fans and practitioners alike. Find the librar of whistlekick books on Amazon by searching "whistlekick books"

We Truly Appreciate You!

Thank you for supporting whistlekick and whistlekick Books. We invite you to visit us at whistlekick.com. While there, you will find links to check out our other books, our store, details about our events, social media, how to leave us reviews, info on our other projects, and much more.

We are always open to your thoughts, questions, and suggestions. You may contact us anytime at books@whistlekick.com.

Thank you!

wK Books